How to Teach
a Love of Reading
Without Getting
Fired

Also by Mary Leonhardt

99 Ways to Get Kids to Love Reading

99 Ways to Get Kids to Love Writing

99 Ways to Get Kids to Do Their Homework

Keeping Kids Reading

Parents Who Love Reading, Kids Who Don't

How to Teach
a Love of Reading
Without Getting
Fired

Published by Devens House, 41 Walnut Street, Devens MA, 01432.

Printed in the United States of America

Design by At Design, Inc. | www.atdesignstudio.com

ISBN 0-9723453-0-2

Acknowledgments

Dedicated to all of my students, who have taught me everything I know about teaching.

Many thanks to Carol Birdsall, for her editing help, Mike Muñoz for his great layouts and graphics, Kim Lapan for her wonderful illustrations, and my husband Dick for his continual support and encouragement.

Contents

Introduction

I started teaching in 1971, in a small Dominican boarding school in California. I spent four peaceful, happy years teaching there: all girls, small classes, no study hall or cafeteria duties, open curriculum, a huge library. I was clueless. I thought that was what teaching was.

Then we moved to Virginia, and I taught in a military school: still small classes but all boys, massive disciplinary problems—almost all of these kids had been kicked out of at least one school before landing there—and a dean of students who didn't believe in ordering paperbacks for classroom use, since, as he put it, "Boys don't like to read anyway." So I was to give them the old boring anthology and assign punishment marching drills and study halls if they wouldn't read it.

But I soon discovered that there weren't enough extra drills to assign to make these kids read the selections in this book. And one day, as they sat dozing over the Carl Sandburg's *Life of Lincoln* selection, the lyrics of a then popular song kept running through my head. I didn't know the title or artist, but these two lines were stuck in my memory:

> *I can't give anymore of my soul away*
> *And still look myself in the mirror everyday.*

I felt as if I had a ball of lead in my stomach. I knew that, by making these kids read essays they, first of all, hated, and, second of all, couldn't even read, I was doing a terrible thing. A cowardly thing. So I made the decision that would control my teaching career for the next twenty-five years. I decided that my first responsibility wasn't to the school, or the dean of students, or even the parents, but to my students. I had to do what I thought was right for them. "Put your anthologies away," I told them. "We're going to the library."

The librarian was a sweet, elderly lady who loved the boys and loved books. So, even though her library was small and dusty, it was wonderful. She had piles of *Boys Life* and *Surfer* magazines. She had a whole section of teenage novels. She had fantasy books, and books about fishing.

"Find something," I told the kids, "and we're just going to sit and read."

The rest of that spring was a revelation to me. The boys brought their books to class, and we sat and read together. That was when I first read *The Outsiders* and *That Was Then, This Is Now* by S.E. Hinton and, along with my students, fell in love with Ponyboy and Mark and Bryan. I started bringing in books I loved from home. The boys started trading books. We were all reading together. I have a vivid memory of a warm Virginia spring day, with the heavy fragrance of flowers outside of the classroom window, and one of my (formerly) worst discipline problems looking up from *That Was Then, This Is Now* and saying, "I don't want the book to end."

The latter part of that school year was wonderful, although, in June, I was told I wouldn't be rehired the following year. Numbers were down, I was told, and they didn't have a position. I assumed they didn't like what I was doing but, son of a gun, I got a call the following autumn from that school with a job offer. More students had shown than expected, and they needed another English teacher.

By then I had another job, but I remember thinking: hmmm. If they didn't fire me after I completely ignored the curriculum, I'm probably safe almost anywhere.

That turned out to be true. I next taught in an inner-city Catholic high school, Norfolk Catholic, filled with kids who couldn't read. I started bringing in comic books, and *Disco Roller Skating* magazines. I also started testing and retesting my students to see what their reading level was. I found that reading anything significantly raised scores, and used this data for my master's thesis in special education. In my more advanced English classes I started letting the kids choose all of their reading, and we spent many happy classroom hours comparing notes on favorite authors. I started reading Dick Francis mysteries, on their advice, but couldn't quite get into the hot new local author, V.C. Andrews (who is still writing to this day, even though she's dead). My students, however, loved her.

But then my husband got out of the Navy, and we moved up to Massachusetts. I began teaching in a wealthy, public, suburban high school. Very different. All of a sudden I had administrators in my classroom, evaluating me all the time. I was expected to teach certain books for certain courses. It was all very organized, and so I gave it a good try. I started assigning my students to read thirty pages a night of *To Kill a Mockingbird*, and *Lord of the Flies*. I became a traditional English teacher, but still kept a little of the spirit of my freewheeling days in Virginia. Instead of assigning all of the students' reading, I usually gave them a three week period for a book of their own choice. They always liked the books they chose better than the ones I assigned. So I started giving them two free reading blocks of time, and then three . . . and then I finally got to the point where I couldn't make myself force the kids to read any assigned books. They read so much more reliably—and enthusiastically—when they chose their own books.

But I wasn't back in my friendly little Catholic school in Virginia, where the administrators believed that if Christ were alive today he would add "Teach the illiterate" to the other works of mercy, such as "Feed the hungry." I was teaching in a very competitive school system, with more administrators running around in my building, I would guess, than in the whole Catholic school system of Virginia. I was also, by now, the mother of three children, and I needed this job.

So I became a little careful. I developed survival techniques. I went underground. I would probably still be happily teaching underground except that by the early 1990's all of the educational "experts" were becoming so loud in national discussions, and saying such stupid things, that I decided that I had to consider all of the nation's school children as my children—not just the kids in my classes. I gathered together all my courage and wrote *Parents Who Love Reading, Kids Who Don't: How It Happens and What You Can Do About It*. In it I pointed out how disingenuous it was of educators always to blame parents for students who hated reading. Maybe, just maybe, forcing endless worksheets on young children, and making older kids read books like *Ethan Frome* and *Great Expectations* had something to do our children's dislike of reading. Schools, I preached, needed to take responsibility for developing avid, independent readers.

With that book, and subsequent ones, I've been invited to travel around the country. Parents and teachers and librarians tell me the same thing, again and again: Schools are drowning in mandated curriculum. Teachers don't dare give the kids time to choose books, and just sit around and read. The whole country seems to be in the absurd position of wanting high reading scores, but not valuing the act of reading enough to give it serious time in the curriculum.

That's what this book is about. I'll share the methods I used to survive during my years of underground teaching. I'll suggest ways of dealing with censorship, and administrators, and parents. I'll offer encouragement.

The first section will list the reasons why you should, as Lady Macbeth says, "Screw your courage to the sticking place," and determine that no student will leave your classroom without falling in love with books. Subsequent sections will deal with various teaching aspects, such as how to set up your curriculum so that you can cover the required work as well as build in a love of reading. Throughout I write in a tip format rather than in a more fully developed essay format, since I know (I really know) how busy teachers are.

If you have any questions or comments, I'd love to hear from you. E-mail is the easiest way to reach me: maryl@tiac.net.

Chapter I

Top Ten Reasons for Teaching a Love of Reading

1.

Only kids who love reading become the excellent, sophisticated readers who score high on standardized tests.

There are no shortcuts in life. Top tennis players are on the court six hours a day, and top readers are absorbed in books for hours a day also. There is a mountain of research that substantiates this. If you're interested in it, a little book by University of Southern California professor, Stephen Krashen, called *The Power of Reading: Insights from the Research* is a good place to start. Or find some kids who have scored very high on the verbal section of the college board exam and ask them how much reading they've done over the last twelve years. You'll find that almost all of the best readers have been, for a good part of their school careers, avid readers.

2.

Avid reading develops the ability to concentrate and focus on class discussions or lectures.

If you've ever taught students in a lower group—and who hasn't—then you know that not only do they know less than students in higher groups, but they can't concentrate or pay attention as well. You're continually putting on dog and pony shows just to keep them with you. I've seen it in every low group I've ever taught—and after thirty years in a classroom, I've taught plenty of low groups. It's the shady little secret that explains why experienced teachers demand high groups. They're easier.

The one common denominator of students in low English groups is a low reading ability. After all of these years I've become convinced that there is something about the act of reading that develops a child's ability to make sense out of oral discussions and lectures. Children learn not only how to process written information better, they learn how to process oral information better.

3.

Kids who read widely become more attuned to the feelings of others.

The major difference between books and videos is that books have narrators who tell us what the characters are feeling. This is a major difference!

Even life doesn't have narrators. In life, or on the screen, we have to guess at inner emotions by what the characters say and do. But in most books we have a narrator who can tell us what characters are thinking and feeling.

I think this is why avid readers are almost always really nice kids. They know that everyone else has feelings, just like they do. I don't have to tell you how much easier it is to teach a class full of nice kids who care about each other.

4. **Book lovers are almost never the ones who disrupt class.**

For one thing, avid-reading kids are most likely paying attention to the lesson, since they can concentrate better. And they are less likely to needle other students, since they understand about feelings. They are also the students who achieve, and so think of themselves as good kids.

I don't think, in all of my years of teaching, I've ever seen a major class disrupter who was an avid reader.

5. **Children who love reading can work independently.**

In children who read that wonderful ability to concentrate comes in. Avid readers usually like doing projects and assignments on their own.

They can easily read the directions and understand the work. With all of their reading, they're used to learning things without adult help. If the work involves a group, that's fine too, because they tend to be gentle kids who get along with their classmates.

A classroom full of avid readers is a dream class, because you can teach them all together, or allow them to work in groups or individually.

6. *Your avid readers will start doing better in all of their subjects.*

Avid reading builds extensive frames of reference. Kids learn about nature, about history, about relationships, about different parts of the country. When you try to teach content about one of these areas, they're ready to learn, because they have a niche in their minds ready for the information.

Most importantly, reading is the key skill in every academic area, with the possible exception of math. Even in math good reading skills will help with word problems.

7. *Students who love reading will keep on reading after they leave your class; you can have a life long influence on them.*

What's the use of teaching, if kids walk out of your classroom, and promptly forget everything you ever said? Facts and figures they may forget, but never a love of reading. If they keep reading, then you've been successful because no matter what else happens, they'll end up well educated.

8. *Teaching will be much more fun and interesting for you.*

Avid readers are always bringing in new books you've never read before. They are full of ideas and can carry class discussions without much teacher help. Their papers are fresh and lively and filled with new insight. You'll find that, every year, you learn as much as they do. Maybe more.

9. *Parents will love you.*

I can't tell you how many parents have told me over the last few years, that the thing about their children's schools that most distresses them is that their children are getting turned off to reading. Parents don't have nearly the urge to make kids read only good literature—or memorize vocabulary words—that teachers have. Most parents understand perfectly well that if a teacher gets a child to read a so-called "good" book, but makes that child hate reading, then the teacher has won a battle but lost the war.

Parents are home with these kids. They see them agonizing over hated books. And they feel really sad that these children they read to, and took to the library, and surrounded with books now hate reading.

For every parent who is nervous about your giving children choice in their reading, you'll have hundreds of parents singing your praises.

10. *You will like yourself better.*

This is the most important reason to lure kids into reading. It's clearly the right, the ethical, thing to do. Kids have to be good readers in this sophisticated, technological society. No one is going to make a good living in a service job any more. Kids who hate reading have all professional doors closed to them.

You went into teaching because you cared about kids, right? I mean, you didn't do it for the money, or the prestige. Let's be serious. You wouldn't be spending your days in a classroom if you didn't care about kids. Do the right thing by them, so you can be proud of yourself. Get them reading!

Chapter Two

Getting Started: An Overview

1.

Resolve to put the interests of your students ahead of the interests of your administrators or fellow teachers, or the community.

Although I am going to teach you survival strategies, you do have to be clear in your own mind about where your allegiance lies. It should lie with your students. This means that you will have to be continually translating and modifying curriculum and school guidelines that are often made for the benefit of everyone but the students.

For example, suppose your principal wants all sophomore English classes taught in exactly the same way so parents aren't always trying to get their kids out of one class and into another. So, in other words, he wants the classes taught in the same way for his convenience: he doesn't want to deal with discontented parents, and he doesn't want to do anything about the teachers who are making the students and parents so unhappy. Let's make everybody unhappy instead!

You simply can't buy into this way of thinking. You can make surface changes that make your class appear to be like the others, but the heart of your curriculum—producing literate tenth graders—has to stay.

2. ***Make your overriding goal be that your students develop a love and habit of reading.***

Make curriculum decisions based on this goal. You'll have secondary goals, too, of course. Just make sure they don't interfere with your primary goal.

For example, my secondary goals are that my students develop the ability to think analytically about their reading, and that they acquire some knowledge and appreciation of our heritage of rich, complex literature. But since these goals are secondary, I only pursue them if they don't put my primary goal in jeopardy. In practice this means that I do very little with my secondary goals when I have a class of turned-off, semi-literate students. In my British and American Literature classes, on the other hand, I can spend a good deal of time introducing classic works, and helping my students talk analytically about them.

3.

When dealing with poor readers, judge books on their ability to lure kids into an educated world, rather than on their literary or cultural merit.

Kids who fall in love with reading, and spend hundreds of hours hunched over their favorite books, will sooner or later tire of formula fiction with stereotypic characters and predictable plots. But let this process happen naturally. If you try to force kids to read books they can't read well— books they are not yet ready for—they'll just end up hating reading. Then they'll never acquire the ability to read rich, complex works of fiction and nonfiction.

If you try to push classics at kids before they are ready, they'll learn to hate them, not appreciate them. Then what have you accomplished?

4.

Be warm, flexible, and loving when dealing with students.

There are lots of reasons to be warm and flexible, but here's the reading one: kids will be more willing to open themselves to books you suggest if they trust and like you.

You will probably have students in your class who have been traumatized by heavy-handed reading instruction. They feel dumb about books. They can never find the main idea, or remember the vocabulary words. Reading, for them, is an activity to be dreaded and avoided. It leads to failing, to being yelled at and punished.

What these kids have no defense against is someone who's nice to them. So try, at all costs and at all times, to maintain your good humor. More later, but for now here is my favorite line when trying to get one of these kids to try a book. I say, "I know that you're a very choosy reader, and don't like just any book. Would you try *The Outsiders* for me? If you like it, I'll figure it's a good book, and other kids might like it too."

5. ***Listen to your students.***

Every good curriculum suggestion I've ever gotten has been from a student. Students have explained to me how they read much more when they can choose books. They've told me how some kids don't mind keeping reading journals, but other kids hate them. We talk about how to structure class discussions, how to do in-class reading, how to organize the week. Besides all of the good advice I get, just the act of asking students for their ideas and opinions makes them feel more friendly and empowered.

A non-threatening way to get feedback is to ask your students to write you an anonymous note every so often describing what works for them in your class, and what doesn't work for them. I usually tell my students ahead of time that I'm going to read their notes out loud to the class, unless they put a note on top telling me not to.

When I read the notes out loud,. I always find that the vast majority of the class is thrilled with the chance to choose their own reading. Hearing this, the few complainers, or the kids who are worried about not having a specific reading assignment every night, decide that maybe it really is okay to settle back and start enjoying a book.

Even if you feel that you can't make the changes students ask for (and often you can't) at least you know what they're thinking, and you know where the mine fields are in your classroom—invaluable knowledge to have.

6.

Spend as much time as you can reading books that you enjoy yourself.

This shows that you value reading. Why would your students believe you when you say reading is important when you sit and correct papers while they're supposed to be reading?

Even more important, it's only avid readers, I think, who really understand how reading works—how readers choose books, what kind of books they like, what kind of assignments motivate more reading—crucial information like that. I believe schools have done a poor job developing a love of reading because so few educators, or policy-makers, love to read themselves.

You'll also find that, just like your students, the more you read the faster and more efficient a reader you'll become. Gradually you're working through your stacks of papers much more quickly.

7. Fill your classroom with books.

All of my students who read have told me, again and again, how easy it has been for them to get books. They have older brothers and sisters who have passed down whole intact mystery or fantasy series. Or they live right by a library. Or they have a wise parent or grandparent who buys them loads of books.

Your classroom should replicate this enriched home environment . You could try demanding a generous classroom library budget, but I think in most school systems this is as effective as spitting in the wind. And, of course, if the school district is paying for the books, your administrators might take an unwholesome interest in the titles that you're ordering.

So see what you can do on your own. You could ask parents for book donations. I do this sometimes on Parents' Night, but most often I just haunt garage sales and flea markets. I can usually get books for a quarter or fifty cents apiece. I like having a wide assortment, because I'm always surprised at a title that will take off. It's often one that I never would have thought to order.

Once I find out that a certain book is wildly successful with students, I'll try to get my department to order five or ten copies. I'll tell them it's for cooperative learning groups . . . or something.

8. *Take every opportunity of throwing support to your school library.*

Somehow the public perception is that computers are essential for school learning, but libraries don't need to be funded. The reality is just the opposite. Books make kids literate, not a computer screen. There will be plenty of time for kids to learn how to use computers, but they need to read right now.

So bring your students to the library, talk with the librarian about good book choices for them, and speak up in faculty meetings in support of an increased library budget. Your respect for the library and librarians will rub off on your students.

9.

Don't worry about all of the time that nurturing a love of reading is going to take.

A while ago I was having lunch with the superintendent of a fairly large school system. When I asked him how much time the children had for free reading, he shook his head regretfully. None at all, he told me. Too much curriculum to cover. Well, maybe the first graders got to read fifteen minutes a day—or was it a week? But everyone else . . .There was just no time.

He was a well-meaning, intelligent man who simply didn't understand how children learn to read. What he said is equivalent to saying that you're in charge of people walking across a desert and, unfortunately, you can't give them any time to stop and drink water. No, they have to design new canteens, talk about various ways of pouring water, get in groups and talk about how to drink water—but, sorry, no time actually to drink!

You'll fight feelings of guilt when you and your class are sitting around happily absorbed in wonderful books. That's okay. We've all been brainwashed. Fight those feelings and let them read.

10. *Most important: Keep an open mind, and always be evaluating and reevaluating how everything is going.*

The tips that follow are the techniques that have worked for me. That doesn't mean that they will work for you. You have your own style, your own strengths and interests. You have to teach in the way that's right for you.

But remember that helping kids fall in love with books is your main goal.

Chapter 3

Motivating Kids: General Tips, So You Can Have a Calm, Productive Classroom

11. *It's critical that your students know that you care about them.*

This is most important for the most unlovable kids. So you need to smile at your students. You need to say hi to them when you see them in the hall. You need to tell them what a wonderful class they are. You need to tell them that you don't want to give them up at the end of the semester.

I have a few lines I use with my most difficult discipline problems: "It's a good thing I like you." Or: "It's a good thing you're such a cute kid." Or: "I'm really worried about you. What can we do that will make this class work better for you?"

You'll be amazed at how an explicit show of caring changes the atmosphere of your classroom.

12. *Get your students to laugh.*

I heard a psychologist, Bart Wendell, comment that if you laugh or cry when learning something it's a "hot cognition." I always try to keep that in mind, and set up situations, or make remarks, that the kids will laugh at and think absurd. Don't ever be sarcastic or mean—just absurd or silly.

For example, one day in my British Literature class we were trying to read Matthew Arnold's "Dover Beach." It was hot out. I could tell most of the class was teleporting to places unknown. So, instead of my reading the poem aloud to them, we went around the room with everyone reading a line. That was pretty funny. Then I realized we needed to stop at the punctuation instead of the line breaks, so we went around again, reading to the next punctuation mark. Some students only read one word. That was even funnier. Pretty soon everyone was awake and laughing. They next wanted to go around with everyone only reading one word, but the bell rang.

Okay, so maybe at that moment they were not learning a lot of British Literature. But they were feeling friendly towards class and towards each other. All of the good physiological things that happen when we laugh were happening (a rise in serotonin levels, that kind of stuff) and, amazingly they even remembered the poem, since a large number chose it as a piece of literature to write about on their final exam.

13.

Be meticulous about treating everyone fairly and politely.

I think it's hard not to like some students more than others, but you simply cannot let that show in a classroom. That's why I like a large part of my grading to be dependent on how much reading each student does: that's an objective measure. During class discussions I keep a running list of the students as they raise their hands, and I call on them in order. That way there is no chance that I overlook anyone.

When students think they are not being treated fairly, discontent starts to spread. Pretty soon, the whole atmosphere of a class can be poisoned. Forget about teaching a love of reading then; you'll be lucky to survive.

14.

The organizing rule is to give up control in the little things, and keep it in the big ones.

For example, as much as possible (more later) you're letting your students choose what they read. I think that's a little thing: who cares what they read? But they must read: that's a big thing. You set up the grading in such a way that they can choose what grade they get for reading by reading a certain amount and having their book with them (again, more later), but the big thing is that they have to do a great deal of reading to get a high grade.

Essentially, you want them to feel in control as much as possible. They'll work better, like your class much better, and be much easier to manage. I know it seems to go against conventional wisdom, but you get control with kids in the important areas only when you give it up in the unimportant ones.

15. *Be very clear with your students about what you consider important issues. You should not have too many of these because these are the things that you won't let slide.*

I need to have my students be honest with me, and be civil to me and to their classmates. They can't lie about what they're reading, they can't hand in someone else's work, and they can't make fun of their classmates or be disruptive so no one else can work. When I ask them to do something, like change their seat, they must comply. Those are my really important issues.

16. *Figure out ahead of time how you'll deal with infractions of important rules.*

You need to figure out a way to react that accomplishes what you want—without depending on the student going along with you.

For example, suppose a girl is telling about a book she's reading that has an unwed mother in it. Some clown yells out, "Yeah, I can see why a slut like you would like that book!" A comment like that is beyond the pale and, if allowed, will ruin morale and order in your classroom. So I'll stand up, eyes blazing, point to the student and say loudly, "Out! Go to the vice-principal's office!" If he doesn't move, I immediately say, "Fine, then I'm leaving now to call him. If you don't leave you'll be insubordinate as well as uncivil, and for that you get suspended." If that doesn't get him out of his chair, I walk across the hall to the English office, and call the vice-principal. The few times I've had to do this, the disruptive student was always gone when I got back to the classroom. If he hadn't left, the vice-principal would have pulled him out.

You might not have the good disciplinary back-up that I do. In that case you need to think ahead of time of something else to do. I think, if at all possible, you have to get that student out of your room for at least a little while, using any way you can think of.

Or suppose that you're pretty sure a student is lying about how much reading she's done. I always say something like, "Alyssa, we need to talk out in the hall for a minute about your reading." Nine times out of ten the student will follow me. If she won't, I say, "Fine, but if you won't talk about it, then I can't give you credit. And, unfortunately, I have to report you to the office as being insubordinate for not following me out into the hall."

Then, when she does follow me out to the hall (she always does) I chat with her about her book and try to determine exactly how much she really has read. I'm gentle with her if it's the first time, and we figure out what kind of credit she can get for the pages she's actually read. But I also point out that she's lied to me and it's going to take a while before I trust her again.

17. *When dealing with serious discipline issues, show only anger or sadness, never contempt or a gleeful "I've got you now!" attitude.*

I'll usually show anger first. "I trusted you and let you choose a book on your own. And now I find out that you really didn't read it? You lied to me?" Then quickly I become sad that the student has misbehaved in this way. Why? What happened? What went wrong? That's what I'll ask. You need to do this so misbehaving students still know you care about them. Otherwise you've lost them forever.

18.

But give your students control over small areas of classroom discipline.

I let my kids wear hats in class, bring food ("zero mess" policy), chew gum, and even put their heads down and take a nap. I figure they can't learn anyway if they're tired. I never refuse permission to go to the rest room or the nurse. If they tell me they're hungry and didn't get breakfast, I let them go to the cafeteria and buy a bagel. If they tell me they're in the middle of a crisis and need to talk to their friend or guidance counselor, I'll say fine and let them go. When they come back, I'm always careful to enquire sympathetically about how they are.

I also try to run some classes as workshop classes, telling the students that on those days they can decide what they want to work on. Maybe they just want to read. Maybe they have writing to catch up on. I drift around lending a hand when they need help; if everyone is working quietly, I get comfortable and read myself. The only golden rule here is that they have to be working on English: no doing history homework.

19.

Do keep control over seating.

I almost always assign seats. It's just too hard for kids to pay attention to their reading, or to you, if they're sitting by their best friend or, God forbid, their boyfriend. Assigned seating also prevents kids in cliques from sitting together, a very bad thing to have happen.

Usually I seat students alphabetically, sometimes by their first name and sometimes by their last name. Then they don't try to figure out who I like, or don't like, or don't trust. I do reserve the right, however, to move someone who can't work peacefully in his assigned seat.

I assign these seats as soon as kids walk in the first day. They sit down, congregating in their little cliques, and then the bell rings. I immediately announce, "I'm assigning seats!" and over their groans and protests, start walking around the room pointing to each desk specifying who is to sit in it. I continue to hear groans but have never had anyone outright refuse. If I did, I'd simply point them to the door and say, "I'm sorry, but I guess you're not in my class then."

20. Don't have all your desks lined up facing front.

I know that this sounds like another small thing, but I don't think it is. You'll want your students to start acting more responsibly and independently by choosing much of their own reading, and by helping their classmates choose books as well. If they are facing each other in a large circle or square—or even in a horseshoe—they'll be more likely to interact.

When I started putting my students in a circle, and making myself part of the circle, I noticed that the whole atmosphere changed. The students were friendlier. They couldn't slump in the back because there was no back. All of a sudden it became possible to have lively book discussions. Most important, there was no longer that "me against them" feeling that sometimes surfaced in a more traditionally arranged classroom.

I know that some teachers feel they don't have as much control over a class that isn't lined up in rows, but I have more of the kind of control I want: a friendly, respectful feeling, an atmosphere conducive to discussion and debate. I don't want the kind of control that has me directing the students' every thought and move.

21.

Negotiate the in-between areas of importance with your students.

Usually this concerns how you're going to deal with the curriculum. I'll give suggestions later for ways to cover required curriculum, but I suggest that you also discuss the ways with your students. Do they like working in small groups? How do they want to do the writing? Which poems of this author should you cover? As much as possible, bring your class in on your planning. Even if you don't think the way they want to do something is as effective as the way you want to, go along, at least at first. Maybe their way really will work out better and, if nothing else, the sense of empowerment they'll get is worth a little inefficiency in covering the curriculum.

22.

Don't call parents until you really have to.

The problem with calling parents for every little homework assignment missed is that you get a short-term gain and a long-term lost. The students will do better at first, but then become so angry over all the calls home, and all the pressure their parents are putting on them, that they'll do even less than they were initially. Some will stop working altogether.

It's much better to handle the situation yourself

for as long as you can. When students misbehave, first try the usual solutions of changing their seats, making sure the work they have to do is interesting and motivating, talking with them, telling them that you're worried about them—I'm sure you know the drill. I'm not much of a believer in punishment—I never make kids stay after school—but you have to do what works for you.

If it's an academic problem, or the misbehavior continues, then I go to Guidance or Special Education. Those counselors and teachers are often really helpful. When things are still deteriorating, and I know I'll have to call the parents, I try to get as much information as I can first. Should we be considering a special education referral? Is the student in a wrong class?

And then, if I still need to call the parents, I always alert the student first. No surprises.

Chapter 4

Teaching the Curriculum

Now that you have your quiet, productive classroom, how do you teach?

23.

Your basic plan will be: required reading in class, independent reading in class and at home.

Luckily, the amount of required reading in a curriculum, over a year, is usually pretty small. In elementary school you might have basal readers with a few chapter books. In junior high you probably are given three or four novels, with a couple of plays or groups of essays. In high school—in a very demanding class—you rarely teach more than four or five books a semester, if that.

I know that the usual procedure is to assign the required reading for homework, and then discuss it in class the next day. I taught like that for years but could never go back to teaching that way now. I had to quiz every day to ensure reading compliance—and even then a good number of kids managed to slip through my net. Even worse, the students who did do the reading often ended up disliking the book. Instead of learning to appreciate a classic, they learned to hate it. The worst thing of all that happened was that, with a required reading assignment hanging over their heads, virtually none of my students did any independent reading at all.

This is how I do the assigned readings now.

24. Do the short readings out loud with your class.

I teach both American and British Literature. The essays, poems, and short stories we read aloud together. I try to do this in a variety of ways, but keep the general principle that, if the students are doing the out-loud reading, they can always just say "Pass" when it's their turn to read.

Difficult poems I usually read to them, and then discuss with them the poem's meaning. For more accessible poems I often divide my students into small groups, and have each group pick a poem to read aloud and explain to the rest of the class. Sometimes, to vary things, I'll call on a student to read a poem aloud, and then ask that student to choose a classmate to explain the poem. Then the classmate that explains the poem chooses another classmate to read the second poem, and so on. This tends to keep everyone alert, worrying about being chosen to explain. I do allow the selected students to select someone else to help them and, of course, the student chosen to read aloud can always pass.

With short stories and essays we usually read a

paragraph each, going around in the circle. If the story has a good deal of dialogue, I'll often assign "parts" to different class members, and read the narration myself. Particularly if the story is comic, this can be a lot of fun. Essays we read in a very leisurely manner, stopping often for comments and criticisms. Usually I don't worry about reading the whole essay; I'll sum up for them the parts we skip.

25. Have students read plays out loud in parts.

With easy, fun plays I usually put the students into small groups so everyone always has a part. If a big room is free during your class period it's good to move the class there, so they can spread out and read without being bothered by other groups. While they're reading, I drift around, listen in, and occasionally ask questions to make sure everyone is following what's going on.

With a more difficult play I'll either keep the class together for the whole play, having kids take turns with parts, or keep the class together for at least the first day of reading, so I'm sure everyone is understanding it.

This year I had a large class with a group that definitely liked reading the plays together in small groups, and another contingent that liked reading in a large group with me. Sigh. So finally that's what we did. About half the class would go down the hall to the Little Theater and sit in groups and read, and the other half would stay in the classroom and read with me. Of course, I'd check up on the Little Theater group every so often, but they seemed to do well.

26. **With novels, first determine if any specific novels actually HAVE to be read.**

Look around your school. You'll probably see some teachers who assign almost no required reading—or any reading—at all. Check out what the absolute minimum is you can do with required novels.

Here's why. Just the fact that a novel is required tends to make kids dislike it, and reading one as a class can eat up weeks of time that could be much better spent having kids read books they enjoy. While it's pretty easy to keep poetry and plays lively and interesting, a long, required novel is a different story.

27. **Use different options for dealing with the novels that are absolutely required.**

Here's what I do in American Literature. *The Great Gatsby* is read by almost all the sections. I explain this to my class, and ask if they, too, would like to read it. I tell them I'll give them a week to do the reading, give them no quizzes or objective tests on it, and suspend the usual weekly reading requirement. I tell them I will want them to do some writing, but they can determine the form. Usually my classes will take this option.

For classes that won't—classes who really do not want to read any book together—I go to Plan B. We read a few sections from the book the way we read short stories, in parts and out loud, and then I form a little group of any students who want to continue with the reading. *Gatsby* will then count as their independent reading, while the rest of the class goes on to other books. And after the *Gatsby* group is done, I'll show the movie to the whole class, and have a general discussion.

I know this isn't perfect, but it seems the least harmful way to go through required novel reading. It keeps your students feeling friendly about reading, and feeling like they're in charge of their reading choices. Ultimately, your students will end up much better readers—readers more likely to choose complex, classic novels on their own.

When I stopped teaching mostly required novels, I was shocked to see how much students dislike most of them. My students didn't tell me at the time—although needing to quiz every day should have been a good clue for me—and I deluded myself into thinking the required reading was going well. It's only now, when I allow almost all independent reading, that my students are telling me how much they dislike the required reading in their other classes, and love to be able to choose in mine.

28. Don't spend lots of time analyzing in-class reading.

The reason you can do almost all the required reading out loud in class is because it's not the reading that takes so much time in a traditional class. It's the peripheral activities. We feel like we have to explain every character, every image, every theme. We put the kids in groups and try to think up creative literary activities. We talk about plot maps and image webs.

The longer I teach, the less I do this kind of stuff. I've found that most students actively dislike so much analysis. It ruins works they were predisposed to like, and I don't find it effective in helping students develop an analytical frame of mind. Students acquire these abilities from wide reading. A thrilling book will pull out of them an understanding of character, an appreciation of theme, the ability to follow complicated plots, and a sensitivity to tone. Stephen Krashen, a University of Southern California researcher, says in his book, *The Power of Reading*, "reading for meaning, reading about things that matter to us, is the cause of literate language development." Your students will be much better prepared to do literary analysis than other students who have sat through endless dog and pony shows.

29. Give open book essay tests on required and independent reading.

You know your students have read the required works—or at least become very familiar with them through a few chapters with summaries and/or videos—so there's no point to testing objective details. No, you want to encourage your students to really think about their reading—to compare books and make connections with the reading they are doing on their own. Give them broad essay topics, let them have all of their books with them, and encourage them to find common themes or literary techniques. You'll be surprised at the quality of work you get. I get so much better writing when I do this, than when I had students all writing essays, or taking tests, on assigned books.

30.

Your students' homework should always be independent reading.

Since you'll be covering required reading in class, you can assign independent reading for homework. You need to assign independent reading, so it has the same weight as other homework your kids get.

This is the heart of your reading program—getting kids to choose books they like, and helping them form a habit of reading outside of class, every day, on their own.

Most of the rest of this book will deal with ways to help this happen.

Chapter 5

Getting Started with Independent Reading

31. *On the first day of class, have your students write a bit about themselves, and then tell you what kind of books they like—or don't like.*

"Tell me the bad news," I always announce. "Let me know what I'm up against." I always keep these little notes. Often you can turn around a real dislike of reading, and it's fun to go back and see how adamant the student was in the beginning.

Problems sometimes turn up in these notes as well, which are good to know about as soon as possible. So read them right away.

32. *After they're finished writing, give them a little pep talk about how important reading is.*

I've found the twin soccer story to work well here. I say to my classes: "Suppose there were a pair of identical twins and one loved soccer and played it all the time, and the other one didn't. One day, for a joke, the twin who hated soccer and never played put on his twin's uniform and walked on the field. How long would it take the coach, or the rest of the team, to realize that the wrong twin was on the field?"

My class immediately tells me that everyone would know right away, because the wrong twin wouldn't know how to pass, how to run, how to dribble the ball—all of the skills that good soccer players acquire. And then I tell them that reading works exactly the same way. Avid readers acquire all kinds of skills that kids who never read don't learn.

33.

Tell your students specifically how much reading you expect from them every week.

Most students coming into your class will be in the habit of doing very little reading. Left to their own devices, they'll think thirty or forty pages a week is a pretty heavy reading schedule. So while you need to take into account the abilities of your classes, I'd suggest you require about two hundred pages a week for an "A," a hundred to a hundred-and-fifty for a "B," and so on down to a "D."

You do this so that you're clear that you expect a good deal of reading, and also so that neither the school administration nor the other teachers can accuse you of not having high standards. I'll bet there aren't any other teachers in your whole school who require two hundred pages of reading a week for an "A." You can only get away with this when your students are choosing books, and you're helping them find books they'll like.

With all but my top classes, however, I tell them that if they're reading a book with small print or large pages, I'll give them a page-and-a-half or two pages of credit for each page. I do this so they choose books on interest, not print size.

Note: This isn't my students only weekly grade. They also get grades for other things, usually involving writing and class participation.

34. ***Tell your students that your most important rule is that they can't keep reading a book they dislike.***

When kids have done very little reading, they think all books are much alike, and all are equally boring. This means they don't bother to look around much for a good book. What's the point? They think the term "good book" is an oxymoron.

So when you see your students reading in a very distracted, bored manner, insist they try another book. And then maybe another. And another. Somewhere out there, tell them, is a book they'll love. They just have to find it. Explain that they'll get credit for a total number of pages read, and the pages can be in many different books.

35.

The other important rule to mention is that they can't count a book they're reading for another class for your class as well.

While it's tempting to let slow readers double dip like this, what ends up happening is that other teachers are dictating what your students read. Slow readers, especially, really need to find high interest books they can't put down, and it's doubtful that that outside reading books for history or science will provide that experience.

This rule is also a statement by you that reading a Stephen King novel or a sports biography is just as important as reading a history book. More important, really, because they'll really read the King novel, and so improve their reading skills.

36.

Explain how you're going to check up on independent reading.

The best way I've found so far is reading journals. I ask my students to keep a weekly journal that lists the pages they've read and, depending on the level of the class, has a short summary or analysis.

Every so often I get a kid who hates writing journals. I try to manage quick conferences with students like this, so they can get credit for reading without having their pleasure ruined by having to write a hated journal.

With younger children you might want to use some kind of parent check-off system. I know that there are programs with computer tests, but I'd avoid them. The choice of books is then limited, and some kids who read the books still fail the tests.

37.

I always start my independent reading assignments with a talk about honesty.

I explain to my classes that, if they want the privilege of choosing books, they have to be honest about the amount of reading they're doing. I point out that I've been doing this for a long time, and— while a kid may slip one or two dishonest journals by me—sooner or later I'm going to catch up with him, and then trust is broken. I won't believe that student again.

I really make a big deal about this, because I find that heads off a lot of problems.

38.

But don't worry too much about kids cheating on reading.

It's really easy to catch kids who lie up the number of pages they've read. You ask them to tell you about their last night's reading. Or you open their book to a page at random, and ask them to describe the scene to you. You'll find that poor readers have an extraordinarily hard time faking reading. They won't be able to answer your questions about the book at all. Plus they do really stupid things like putting the same pages down, week after week, or claiming that they read two hundred pages in *The Old Man and the Sea*. (Just the fact that a poor reader is claiming to have read a book like that is suspicious, especially when he clearly has no idea how long the book even is.)

Really good readers can fake reading a book— but if they're allowed to choose books, why would they fake it? They're good readers because they read all the time. This is just a golden opportunity for them to continue to do what they like—read.

39.

Think about giving a weekly grade on in-class reading behavior as well.

I've just started doing this with my sophomores, and it's very effective. I tell my students that if they have their book with them every day, and if they quietly read when they get reading time, then they get an "A" for in-class reading for the week. If they don't do as well, their grade is lower.

This is an "A" that even slow readers can get, which makes the grade very popular, and discourages complaints from parents and students about the large number of pages needed for an independent reading grade of "A." You can make it count for any part of their grade you want; even if it counts little there's something magic in an "A."

Chapter 6

Helping Kids Choose Books

40. *Allow class time for choosing books.*

You're going to have lots of books (or magazines or comics—or whatever you think will work) in your classroom. In addition, you should have checked out the library and have some idea what's available there. Then make sure all of your students have reading material to take home and read.

Once in a great while I'll let a few students tell me that they already have books at home that they're reading. But I don't like to do this, because often they don't have books at home—or don't like the ones at home, or can't find them. So I usually say something like, "That's great you have a book at home. But why don't you find one now just to read for the rest of class. Then you can switch to your at-home book if you want to." I say this because usually a book that a student finds with my help ends up more appealing than the unread book sitting at home.

41. *Put as few restrictions on book choice as possible.*

For example, I tell my students in American Literature to choose books by American authors, and give them a book list for reference. They don't have to stick to the book list; it's just for suggestions. I do the same with British Literature. My sophomores can read anything.

But I really discourage you from telling your students that they can't read series books, or all books by the same author, or horror books—or any books that you, personally, don't like. Kids have to start somewhere and usually the books that we teachers don't like are the very ones to help a student fall in love with reading.

42. *Even when your curriculum seems to demand a certain kind of outside reading, be flexible with individual kids.*

The only class this becomes a real issue for me is in British Literature. It's supposedly a high level course and should have only students who can enjoyably read books that are a bit complex. But you know how it goes. I always get a few students who can't even get absorbed in authors like Jack Higgins or Rosamunde Pilcher. So I will quietly tell them just to find any book they like, and we'll think of a way to make it British. And this year one of my best students liked European literature better but, he gravely informed me, the translators were British.

In my sophomore courses, even when they are labeled something like "Mystery" or "Coming of Age" I allow any kind of reading. After all, there's a little mystery in every sports book, right? Most fantasies also contain some kind of mystery. And any book that has a character solving a problem or learning something is a coming-of-age book.

It's interesting to me that even though I am very public about allowing this kind of leeway with my sophomores, most don't take advantage of it, but read books that fit solidly into the curriculum. As with British and American Literature, I give out suggested reading lists, and a majority of the students really use them.

43. *When helping kids who don't like to read choose books, ask them either to tell you the name of a book they've read and really liked or—if they tell you they've never liked any book—to tell you about an activity they enjoy.*

In one of my longer books, *Keeping Kids Reading*, I go into great detail about the reading paths different readers take. The short version is this: kids usually like either relationship books or action/adventure books. Within those two broad categories they usually prefer either realistic, or more imaginative books. The less sophisticated a reader is, the fewer books that reader will initially enjoy. So while an avid reader will usually prefer a certain kind of book, but happily read almost anything, a beginning reader will only want to read a certain kind of book.

For example, if a boy tells you that the only books he's ever liked are books about hunting, you'll want to suggest a book by a writer like Gary Paulson, who writes outdoor adventure type books. A boy who has never read a book he liked, but who plays sports, should start with some kind of sports fiction or non-fiction. There's Matt Christopher for younger readers, and much non-fiction for older ones. A girl who loves realistic relationship books will like Judy Blume or Mildred Taylor. One who likes more imaginative books (usually with happy endings) will like writers like E.B. White, or Maud Hart Lovelace. Almost everybody (myself included!) likes the Harry Potter books. I think Rawlings has managed to write books that have relationships, action/adventure, fantasy, sports, realism, and even comedy.

44. *If kids can't seem to find a book on their own, you'll have to help.*

I always have a couple of students who read the first few pages of a number of books (ten! fifteen!) before settling down and finishing one. When students are truly trying to find something they can read, and seriously reading at least several pages per book, I let them alone. Their reading journals are funny: they carefully list ten pages here and twelve pages there. And that's okay. I find they sooner or later finally get hooked, and read a book all the way through.

It's the kids that really don't seem to be trying that you have to worry about, the ones who spend all of their time at the bookshelves fooling around, and never really committing to even trying a book. After a day or two of this, I hand each one several books and say, "Read the first three pages of each, and then pick one to read today. If you don't like it you can switch tomorrow, but try it for today."

Since I teach high school, my choices for these kids may be different from yours. For high school students, I give these battle-weary, burned-out, hostile readers books by R.L. Stine (the Fear Street series), Robert Parker (the Spenser novels), S.E. Hinton (her earlier books), V.C. Andrews, Judy Blume—anything I have handy that is easy to read and full of action.

45.

If no books in your classroom seem to work, send your reluctant reader to the library with a reading classmate with similar tastes.

The majority of my hardest-to-get-reading boys like sports, so I encourage them to go with a friend who has already read some sports books. The friend will know where the books are, for one thing, and can give some recommendations. Certain books will then sweep my sports-reading boys.

46.

Throughout the book-choosing process, emphasize that everyone has different tastes, and that's okay.

I tell my class as a whole that they'll like different books, and I repeat that to individual students, especially ones who are having trouble finding books. You do this for two reasons: one, because it's true, and two, because most kids who think they don't like reading just haven't liked the books they've been assigned in school. You want to keep telling them that of course they like reading; they just haven't found the right book yet. No one, tell them, likes every book.

47.

The initial books that kids choose may really floor you; that's okay.

I had a student last year who told me that he hated to read. Okay: I moved into my standard patter. Had he ever read a book he liked? No. Well, what kinds of things did he enjoy doing. Sports? No. Outdoor adventure? No.

"Well," I persisted, "what do you like?"

"I like fixing tractors," he told me. "I live on my grandmother's farm, and I like fixing tractors."

A tough one. I didn't know of any books that dealt with fixing tractors. "Well," I said vaguely, "why don't you go and look around the library."

He came back with a book on the Three Mile Island nuclear meltdown. I gulped and lied, "It really looks interesting!"

His journal that Friday raved about the book. "It has everything, suspense, facts . . ." It was the first book he had ever liked. When he finished it, after describing all of the horrors in loving detail in his journal for me to read, he got out a book on Chernobyl, which he also loved. And then he got out another . . . The last time I chatted with him he told me he was planning a career in nuclear power.

I guess the moral of this story is to keep an open mind. You just never know what that magic book will be that will unlock an interest in reading.

48.

A day or two after your students have started reading independent books, have them take turns telling a little about their books to the rest of the class.

You do this so kids who are poor readers—and aren't really planning to do this reading-at-home business—will see that much of the class is jumping right into books, and seems to be enjoying the reading.

Since I always have my classes sitting in a circle, I just go around the circle asking for a sentence or two summarizing their reading so far. You want this activity to move quickly at first. I think it works best to do this at the end of the first or second day of in-class independent reading, so everyone will have something to say.

As we progress around the room, I usually interject some comment about how interesting it is that most people are liking different kinds of books.

49.

Be sure to emphasize that when students finish a book ("Oh, that's wonderful! You're such a great reader!") they should immediately look for another one. ("But what are you going to read next?")

This always comes as a little surprise to many kids, who have been used to having a book assigned, reading it (maybe), and then relaxing for a week or two until some other reading assignment comes along. But you want them to get into the habit of reading one book after another—or even two or three books at the same time.

Because always having a book going, always being on the lookout for another great book, is the real hallmark of an avid reader.

Chapter 7

Day to Day

50. *At the beginning of the semester, or year, allow as much time as possible for independent reading in class.*

In junior high or high school, for example, I think you should try to dedicate the whole period, every day for the first week, to independent reading. In elementary school, see if you can take all the time allotted to reading instruction for the first week. You're trying to establish a reading habit, and you are also signaling that you think pleasure reading is so important that you're willing to give a whole week just to it.

This time also gives you a chance to see where the problems will be: the kids who can't settle to a book, the kids who can't find one they like, the kids who cut off to the cafeteria on the library pass you wrote for them. Be very encouraging but firm with your students this week. You are so proud of the way they quietly read! Remember that everyone who is quietly looking at a book for this reading time will get an "A" for in-class reading behavior. Let's see if the whole class can get an "A"!

51.

During the first week, also have the students write a couple of sentences in their reading journals every day, giving the number of pages read and a bit of summary.

You need to read these every night for this first week. Don't grade them. In fact, I tear through them, writing things like "Good start!" or "Wow, lots of reading!" or "This book really sounds good." Something inane and encouraging. Then pass them back at the beginning of the period the next day, and tell them you'll collect them again at the end of class. This really helps to keep them focused and reading.

52.

You can teach your regular curriculum after the first week, but maintain some class time for independent reading.

I used to designate specific reading days, but this last year, in my sophomore class, I started making the first fifteen minutes every day be quiet reading time.

My students came in, and I said, "Okay, sit down now and read your books. I'm just going to drift around and make sure everyone has something to read." Then I walk around and see what everyone is reading. It's a good, quick check to make sure they really are reading what they say they are, and it gives me a chance for a few quick words of support to individual students.

The fifteen minutes a day worked very well. Almost all of my students were really reading all of the time—and I had some very difficult non-readers. Reading every day meant they always had to have a book with them (or look for one on my shelves) and they got in the habit of daily reading. Many of the students carried the book right along to their study periods, and continued reading.

For my more advanced classes I've been designating one day a week as a reading day. That has worked well for most of the students, but I always have a couple who end up using that time to find another book—which lets me know that they haven't been reading regularly for the rest of the week. Consequently, this year I'm going to try the every day fifteen-minute-period with them too.

Again, even though it's very tempting for you to use this time to grade papers, I think it's important you read along with your class. You aren't going to allow your students to do other homework during this period—a thing they'll try, thinking reading can't possibly be as important as their math homework—and I don't think you should either.

53.

Every couple of weeks, spend at least a period hearing longer reading reports from your students.

I do this in a variety of ways. Sometimes we just take turns going around the circle, with everyone catching the class up on the latest reading. This way is fine if you have an interested, compliant class. Encourage questions and discussions. Perhaps there is so much discussion that not everyone gets a turn. That's fine. Just continue the next day. This is my favorite way to hear reading reports, because it's relaxed and somewhat like a regular literary discussion.

But with a more difficult class this way sometimes doesn't work. The kids don't listen to each other. They get bored and impatient easily. With a class like this I keep the reports very short—a minute or two—and ask for a rating of the book after the report. Usually we do a scale of one to ten. You can have someone at the board keeping track of books that get a nine or ten rating.

Or, for variety, I'll have one student give his report, and then have that student choose the next student to go. Or I'll put the kids in groups of two, and have them confer and then report on each other's book. Or I'll have them write ad copy for their book and then read it to the class. Try any gimmick that gets them listening to each other.

What happens is they hear their classmates being enthusiastic about books and about reading. They'll decide to try the book their friend is reading. Pretty soon books start to sweep the class. They start asking each other for recommendations.

54.

Avoid having kids do elaborate presentations on their independent reading.

I know, I know. Somehow getting a kid up in front of the class with his accurate, scaled model of a bunny from Watership Down is the height of good teaching—right up there with curriculum-loaded bulletin boards and presentation software. But personally I think all of that is a waste of time. I'd rather have the kid spending his time reading. Here's why.

There's a good chance the pressure of a big presentation will take all the enjoyment out of reading. And there's an equally good chance that the parents will be there constructing the bunny, or software, right along with him. What's the point?

Plus, what might be at least marginally interesting to other kids who have read the same book, is deadly boring to kids who have no idea what he's talking about.

55.

Start identifying students as experts in certain kinds of literature.

Suppose you have a boy who used to hate reading, but now is reading sports books. That's great! Be sure to refer other kids to him who are looking for a sports book they'd like. Ask him seriously, during class book discussions, what the best basketball book is. Or soccer book. Have your Stephen King readers dispense advice on the best King book for someone just starting to read horror.

You do this for the good advice they can give, but mainly so that they begin to see themselves as intelligent, literate people.

56.

Consider starting book club groups if you have a class with pretty accomplished readers.

The book club idea is a nice way to ensure that students can choose books, but can also discuss a favorite book with other classmates. But I caution you to do this only with good readers. Poor readers are too individualistic in the books they like, and read at too slow a speed to keep up with other readers. Plus, even a book club book starts to seem like required reading to them, and pretty soon they're doing all of the things they've always done to avoid reading an assigned book: they're asking their friends what it's about, they're watching the movie—or they're just sitting, slumped, in the back of the reading circle.

Even with good readers you have to be careful about the book chosen. Make sure it's short and interesting, so all the members will really read it. I do think book clubs should always be optional. Your students should always have the choice of just reading whatever they want.

57. *When certain books become class favorites, be sure to send some students to the library to request that the librarian order other books by that author.*

You do this to get the books made available, of course, but also to help familiarize your students with how helpful librarians are. There's a good chance your school librarian will be able to suggest a similar book to your students, to tide them over until the new one comes in.

Actually, any excuse to get your kids into the library is good. Avid readers hang around libraries. You want your students to do that too.

58. Work your students' independent reading into your curriculum whenever you can.

Suppose you're teaching your students how to write fiction. Start the lesson with a discussion of books they're reading that they really like. Start talking about what elements of the books makes them so enjoyable. Brainstorm a list for the board. Or supposed you're trying to teach some great classic literature like *Romeo and Juliet*. Ask them about other love stories, or growing-up stories, they've read. How have they ended?

The ability to do this is one of my favorite things about having my students do so much independent reading. When I was teaching all assigned novels, I couldn't get going a good, free-ranging discussion that involved lots of books. My classes would sit looking dully at me when I tried—because, I now realize, they hadn't read anything but assigned books for years and years. (Back then, I still had the vague idea that kids were doing pleasure reading outside of class, on their own. Not.)

Now we have a wonderful time, bringing together all kinds of different books and authors.

59. *With all but your top classes, allow one day a week for in-class journal writing, or quick book conferences.*

You can do this with your top classes too, if you like, but you have to do it with your mediocre or low ones. You want them to succeed. You want them to get credit for the reading they are doing. So devote the same day each week—I use Fridays—to quiet reading and journal writing. The idea is that they write about whatever they read that week, and get whatever credit that is worth. Or they see me for a quick conference.

If kids are out sick, of course, I let them hand in the journal the following week. But generally it's not a good idea to take late journals. Students who don't hand in journals usually have not done much reading. They think that somehow, magically, the next week they'll do double the amount of reading, but that rarely happens. Usually they just get further behind with journals, and then become tempted to cheat, and claim reading that they haven't done.

My general rule is that kids can read ahead and bank pages for the following week, but they can't catch up unless they were sick. I do bend the rule for really problem readers, sometimes just averaging what they've managed to read over however many weeks they're missing a journal entry. But I try not to do it too often because I really want them to get in the habit of turning in weekly work.

60. *Try to get the journals back to the kids as soon as you can—the next class day if possible.*

I know how hard this is, but I think it's more important for kids to get it right back with a grade for the pages they read and a grade for their general reading effort, than for you to do a meticulous job editing every entry. Do a little editing if you want to, but basically just react to what they're reading, with encouraging comments.

61. *With classes that are heavy with traditional curriculum, try to arrange separate, out-of-class reading conferences with each student.*

The idea is that in curriculum-heavy courses, like a British Literature course, you never have as much class time as you'd like for free-ranging book discussions. In these courses I try to schedule one or two conferences each quarter with every student. We sit and chat about their reading, their writing, and what direction they'd like to go next. The personal attention helps the students feel friendlier about class, and reading, and the contact helps me have a better sense of how things are really going in class.

I can usually manage these conferences because

I teach only four classes out of seven periods. If you teach five, and have a huge student load, than I doubt that it's possible. It's barely possible for me with four.

Chapter 8

Book Discussions

62. *Tell your class you would like to have a free marketplace of ideas, but that only works if everyone agrees to maintain a civility of discourse.*

Suppose, I explain, that I tell you that short people are smarter than tall people. Since I'm only five feet, two inches, that has always seemed like a reasonable thesis to me. In a free marketplace of ideas, you would have to right to disagree. You might say something like, "But Mrs. Leonhardt, have you ever considered that Abraham Lincoln was over six feet tall—and he was really smart?" That's fine. What's not fine is to personally attack me, and say something like, "How can you be such an idiot to believe something like that?" That's breaks civility of discourse.

Then I ask my classes if they will sign a statement agreeing to maintain civility of discourse so we can have a free marketplace of ideas. I explain that if they get so angry that they're afraid they'll lose control, they can get up and go to the cafeteria and get a cold drink.

In the ten years or so I've been doing this, I've never had a class refuse to sign that statement, I've only had one student go for the cold drink, and I haven't had more than a handful throw out a personal insult. The concept has really worked for me.

The idea is to make your classroom a place that's safe for kids.

63. Don't be afraid to let the discussion veer off into tangents.

Suppose you're talking about what makes an interesting villain in a book. Everyone is talking about the characters in their books who do bad things, and the discussion starts centering on the issue of whether or not contemporary villains are likely to be more insane than evil. That's great, you're thinking. A really solid literary discussion is actually happening in your class!

Then a girl in the back puts up her hand and says that her coach is insane because she makes the team do so many stupid fitness drills. Another hand shoots up and the student complains that his coach is always yelling at them. Should you drag the discussion back to literary villains? Or go with the flow?

In this case, I'd probably use the new direction of the discussion as an opportunity to talk a bit about what mental illness really is. If the class wouldn't be pulled, then I'd let it drift back to a discussion of coaching practices, (not allowing it, of course, to focus on the individual coach) on the principle that any discussion that had my students articulating ideas, listening to each other, and feeling that what they had to say was important would eventually bear fruit. The real purpose of discussions, after all, is to get your students thinking, right?

64. *Try not to comment too much during class discussions. You don't want your students looking to you for right opinions. It's better they hash out things themselves.*

This is hard sometimes, when students say outrageous things. I remember one year, when the AIDS epidemic was at its height, a girl telling the class that the disease was a punishment from God. Another student pointed out that apparently monkeys first had the disease and it somehow got transmitted to humans. The girls jumped right back with, "See, it's a punishment for having sex with monkeys!"

I sat back, barely breathing, waiting to see if civility of discourse would hold. It did! Other students gravely, and politely, explained about virus mutations, while disagreeing with her idea of AIDS as a divine punishment. She listened, restated her opinion, and everyone finally agreed to disagree. At the end of the semester, she wrote on her course evaluation that the best thing about the class for her were the discussions.

I learned from that experience that when students feel that their opinions are respected, they are very willing to listen, and consider, the opinions of others. Even if they are not convinced by others, they have at least tacitly admitted that there is another side to the issue.

65. *Use lots of praise.*

Okay, I'm shameless here. Almost no matter what a student says, I'll say something like, "That's a really interesting idea. I'd never thought of that before."

I also am always throwing in comments like, "It's so great you've read all those books about underwater demolition and can add this interesting information to the discussion."

What you're trying to do is make your students feel like literate, interesting people who enjoy sitting around talking about books.

66. *The only kind of comment I don't allow is criticism about books that students haven't read.*

Once students have read a book, they can say anything they want to about it. But I don't think it's fair to let kids make disparaging comments about books they haven't even tried, comments which will just discourage kids who would like those books from trying them.

You're going to have students reading love stories and books about prize fighting. The last thing you want is for the girl reading a love story to say, "That book on fighting looks awful! How can you read something like that?" The minute kids become embarrassed about their choices you're in trouble. They'll try to read "safe" books, and will end up not really reading at all.

You have to understand that kids who don't like to read assume that any book they might enjoy will really seem dumb to everyone else. They have no confidence at all in their reading choices. It's your job to make them feel comfortable reading the kind of books that will lure them into a literate world.

Chapter 9

Fun Every-so-often Events to Do

67. *Try putting on Oprah shows in a class that's heavy with required reading.*

This is a way to make the required reading that you're doing together with your class a little more interesting. I've done it with a lot of periods and authors, but the funniest turned out to be our Chaucer Oprah show.

I took a group of volunteers out in the hall, and we planned it out. Someone was Oprah, someone was the Wife of Bath, The Prioress and so on. We decided the gig would be that the Wife of Bath had just published a book titled: *How to Control Men.* Then we went back in to our "studio audience" and everyone acted their part, with much funny dialogue going on between the characters and the Wife over her suggestions.

I've done American Lit. ones too, with old authors coming back and giving advice to current authors the kids are reading. One year I coached "Ben Franklin" to simply say a maxim, no matter what he was asked. So "Stephen King" might say, "Well, Mr. Franklin, why didn't you ever write fiction?" and "Franklin" would reply "A penny saved is a penny earned."

What kids get out of these classes is a greater familiarity and enjoyment of famous authors, as well as experience play-acting. And we always laugh a lot.

68.

Try playing trivia when you want your students to have some specific, detailed knowledge.

Divide the room into two teams, and have each team make up questions (on whatever you're reviewing) for the other team. I usually give out slips of paper and have everyone write three questions. Then each team's questions go into a different box, which I take.

I start by drawing out a question from one team, and asking it to the first member of the other team. If that player gets the right answer, the team gets two points. A player who doesn't know the answer can go for a team answer, and if anyone on the team can answer the question, the team gets one point.

At this point, the other team can challenge the answer. (This is to keep the other team paying attention). If someone challenges a correct answer, the first team gets double points. If a wrong answer goes unchallenged, the first team gets the points anyway. And if a wrong answered is challenged and corrected, then the second team gets the points.

This is also a game that usually ends up being funny, since kids pick odd details to ask questions about.

69. *Have a panel of students judge group poetry presentations as if they were a diving or skating event.*

Appoint a panel of judges from the class and, while the rest of the class are in little groups figuring out how to present their poem, take the judges out in the hall and prep them. Have them make number cards to hold up—a presentation might get an 8.5 for example—and then have them decide what country they represent.

Sometimes I tell the judges to judge seriously, and sometimes I tell them to be absurd. The silly ones are the most fun. The judge from Ireland, for example, might mark down a presentation because the poem didn't have any green imagery in it. One year one judge wanted to be from the Vatican. He judged on whether poems had a "holy seven" and other unexpected things.

These are the poems the kids seem to remember.

70.

Start a theme discussion, that incorporates class and independent reading, with a class survey.

For example, if we're going to be talking about how the possession of wealth is viewed by authors, first I'll put categories of wealth on the board, from "Living on the Street" to "Obscenely Rich." Then I'll ask the kids in which group are they most likely to live happy, productive lives. ("Upper Middle Class" usually wins.) Then we make a list on the board of the books the class is reading, and see where each author comes down on the question.

What is really interesting is that sometimes it's in the more classic books, like Jane Austen's, that wealth is seen as leading to happiness, whereas many modern authors view wealth as leading to corruption.

71.

Pretend your School Board is going to decide whether certain works of literature can be in the curriculum, and special interests groups show up at the hearing to argue.

Appoint some students to be on the Board, and have the rest of the class sign up for such special interest groups as the Feminists, the Marxists, the Conservative Religious Believers, the English Professors, and the Students Against Boring Literature. Then have each group argue to the board what books students should and shouldn't read.

The feminists, for example, don't like *The Great Gatsby* because the women in it are either weak and silly, or liars. Marxists think the book shows up the corruption of the upper classes, and so like it. Religious readers object to the total lack of any values shown by the characters, English professors love it for the rich imagery, and the Students Against Boring Literature think it's, well, boring. As one student said, "If you can't understand it while you have a hangover . . ."

I really like to do this, because I think kids then become aware that people judge literature on different criteria. I tell students that that's all right; they just need to be aware of the basis of evaluation.

And I think this exercise also arms them against insensitive people making fun of their reading choices. They can just think, oh well, that must be an English Professor type.

72. *Use famous lines as story beginnings.*

After you've finished reading a play or some poetry together, have the students write down three of their favorite lines from the work. Put all of the slips with the lines on them into a box and divided the class into groups of three or four each.

Pass the box around and have each student draw out three lines.

Now pass out sheets of paper, and announce that everyone should use one of the three lines as the opening of a story, and should write on the story for five minutes. At the end of five minutes tell everyone to stop writing, and to pass the paper around their group to the left. After everyone in the group has had a chance to write five minutes on each group story, have the group reread each story to see which is the best. Then have them read the story to the class.

My students love this exercise because the stories are so funny; I like it because it makes them more familiar with famous lines, while giving them an enjoyable writing experience.

Chapter 10

Working with Special Ed. Students

73.

Free-choice reading, with the major curriculum work covered in class, will make mainstreaming special ed. students much easier for you.

Now you don't have to worry about finding a novel that the whole class can read. The difficult reading you are doing together. No longer will sped tutors be summarizing books for your students. Now you will have the students really reading.

I've also seen that Attention Deficit kids do much better in the classrooms I run now. They calm down and concentrate better when so much of what they're reading and writing is their own choice, and when they are being empowered to make so many little decisions themselves.

74.

You are probably going to have to give pep talks to your sped kids because they will come in thinking they can't do the regular reading.

Every so often I get a student who says to me, "I can't read; I'm dyslexic." I explain that being dyslexic means you have to read more, not less.

I tell them to pretend for a minute that tennis

were as important to future success as reading is—and they weren't very coordinated. "You'd just have to practice and practice," I tell them. "You'd never be great, but if you practiced enough you could play a decent game. It's the same with reading, except that reading well is crucial for later life. And you will be able to read well. You just have to practice more."

75. *Don't reduce the number of pages your special education students need to read to get a certain grade.*

As long as you set up your grading so that everyone can get at least a "C" with a reasonable amount of effort, I'd hold fast to the greater number of pages kids need to read to get an "A" or a "B". I require fifty pages for a "C" and in the classes that have a significant number of special ed. students I usually give plenty of in-class reading time. With the in-class time, the homework time, and the ability to choose any interesting book, I don't think fifty pages is too much to ask.

This problem arises because some special ed. students think the work needs to be arranged so they can get an "A". Well, they can get an "A" if they read two hundred pages. Yes, it will take a lot of time—but what better thing could they be doing with their time? If they don't somehow pick up the ability to read fast and fluently, their future options are greatly limited. I don't think an ed. plan is going to help them avoid reading in college and the workplace.

76. ***Do be sympathetic and helpful with their special problems.***

Suppose you have a boy who is a very poor reader. Go all out to help him find easy, interesting books. Tell him to remember to ask you if some pages can count as more than one page. (Okay: so I fudge a little here with very poor readers.) I've even allowed graphic novels (i.e. bound comic books) sometimes. If you're teaching in an elementary school I'd definitely allow comic books, picture books, joke books—any kind of books that get kids reading.

I think you'll be surprised, though, to see most special ed. kids rise to your challenge. They are usually so glad to be treated as a regular student.

77. ***Don't count books on tape as reading.***

I'm probably standing alone on this issue, but I think having students listen to books on tape instead of reading a book is one of the worst things that's come along. Other teachers tell me that the kids follow along with the narrator and read the words to themselves. Right. Sell me some land in Florida too.

I'd much rather have a girl who reads poorly read an *Archie* comic herself than listen to someone else reading *Pride and Prejudice* on tape. Listening to tapes doesn't produce good readers.

78.

Don't look at computers as the magic bullet for disabled learners either.

Computers are great for some things: writing, especially, and math and science. And while kids do a certain amount of reading while surfing the net, I think they're mostly downloading music and playing games.

If anything, I find that avid readers do very well with computers, and poor readers do not. So the reading needs to come first.

Chapter 11

Working with Gifted Students

79. *A classroom allowing much independent reading works much better with gifted children as well.*

Finally they can go wild and just read all of the things they want to—and get credit for the reading. They will also be your most grateful students since I've found that my gifted kids were usually the most unhappy in traditional classrooms.

Part of the set-up of my classes is that students can bank pages if they read ahead. Avid readers go wild with this, banking hundreds—sometimes thousands—of pages. Theoretically that means they can take off a few weeks and not read at all, but they rarely do that. They just keep accumulating extra pages after extra pages.

80. *Utilize your gifted kids, especially in a heterogeneous class, to spark up the teaching of the traditional curriculum.*

Gifted kids can be very funny. Last year one of the brightest kids I've ever taught volunteered to illustrate Jonathan Edward's sermon that we were reading in American Lit. As you may know, it's a very scary sermon; Edwards compares sinners to spider's prey, dangling over hell fire. This student made the whole thing hysterically funny with his drawings, and that class was one of the most memorable of the semester.

81.

Also utilize your gifted kids to let other students see how much better they could be in reading.

Most poor readers don't realize how poorly they read. They think it takes everyone an hour to read ten pages. They are shocked, floored, the first time they hear their classmates give reading reports, and hear that some kids have read two or three books during the last week. At first they assume the kids are lying but after hearing gifted kids talk about their reading it's impossible to believe they haven't read the books.

This gives your sports analogy much more credibility. Practice really does increase performance. And it also lets your struggling students see that maybe the problem isn't that they're dumb. Maybe the problem is that they don't read nearly as much as the more advanced students. I know this is obvious to you, but not to kids.

82. *If you have a whole class of gifted students, resist the temptation to begin assigning specific books again.*

It is very tempting, when everyone reads well, to make everyone read a common novel, so you can have great discussions. But still, some kids won't like the book. Others won't bother to read it carefully (really!), and others won't read it at all—just because it's assigned. They'll read the Cliff Notes or watch the video. Just because they're kids, just because they're ornery, and just because they can't believe a book a teacher would assign would be worth their while.

What you can do with these students, however, is book clubs. They are great at finding like-minded classmates, and doing some really serious reading with them. They are also great at free-wheeling discussions that deal with lots of books.

Chapter 12

Working with Parents

83.

Explain your independent reading program to parents on back-to-school night.

I usually give the same handouts to the parents that I've given to the kids. I explain how we're going to cover the traditional curriculum, and how I'm going to structure independent reading.

The thing here is to be aware that many parents are defensive about reading since most people believe that if you read to children every night, and take them to the library, and read yourself, that they'll grow up to love books. You'll have parents who did all those things, and still ended up with kids who hate to read. So you need to start off by assuring parents that you know they've done lots of things to get their kids reading; you're just going to help a little.

84.

First talk about how important independent reading is.

I usually tell stories about my most successful students, all of whom are independent readers. I tell the parents that, by high school, a love and habit of reading are the distinguishing characteristics of excellent students. I list for them all of the reasons for nurturing reading that I listed at the beginning of this book. I also tell them stories of students who started out hating reading, but got turned around and became avid readers. Tell them it's never too late to turn kids into avid readers.

I think you'll find that almost all the parents immediately agree with you. In fact, you'll have much more success convincing parents of this, than your colleagues or administrators.

85. *Explain your policy on censorship.*

My policy is that parents can censor what their own children read, but not what other children read. So they are perfectly free to prohibit their children from reading Stephen King novels—but there is no way I'm going to pull his books from my shelves and deny other children the opportunity.

And I think you'll find with virtually all parents this is good enough. I've found that most of the parents who go to war over books in the curriculum are upset that their children are being made to read a book they disapprove of. Even if they can get their children excused from that assignment—and most schools will allow an alternate book—their child is left in the socially precarious position of being the only one in the class not allowed to read a certain book.

Point out that when children are all choosing books, the situation is completely different. A child who can't read a certain book isn't stigmatized, because none of the other kids in the class even know about the prohibition.

86. Offer to help steer certain kids away from certain books at a parental request.

I always tell parents that I understand that there might be compelling reasons why a certain child should not read a certain book. Perhaps issues are raised in that novel that the child is not prepared to face now—for whatever reason. I find that parents often have very good reasons for wishing to keep their children away from certain authors, and I'm happy to help them do that.

You do have to warn parents, however, that sometimes just forbidding a book will make it more desirable. You'll do what you can, but because your policy is that students can choose any book, the parent will have to be the one to absolutely forbid it.

But I rarely run into this as an issue. The kids I have are in high school, and by then most parents are just so happy to have their kids reading that I almost never get complaints. The few times I have, the students have pretty much taken care of it themselves. ("What do you mean, I can't read that book?! And leave my teacher alone. I'm embarrassed to have you coming in school!")

87. ***Point out to parents that it's really helpful if they take their kids to bookstores or libraries, and help them find books.***

Realistically, with library budgets cut so much, young reluctant readers often do better in a book store. Suggest to parents that money invested in books is better than money invested in a savings account for college. What good is college money going to do if the kid can't read well?

My other favorite line is to ask parents how much they spend on sports equipment a year. If they have a hockey player, they're spending well over a thousand, with league fees and equipment— not to mention traveling and summer camps. Even a soccer player will cost a thousand if she's in a full program.

So tell your parents: spend a thousand a year on books for your children.

88.

If you do get a few parents who are really trying to make trouble for you, dig in and don't give up your program.

Why should a few parents be able to ruin a good reading program for everyone else? Don't let them. Be brave. Believe me, other parents are seeing that their children are happily reading for the first time. If push comes to shove, they'll come to your aid. Hey, with low reading scores across the country, most parents will want to give you a medal. Almost all of the parents who talk to my principal are asking that she over ride their children into my already full classes. I have had a few complainers over the years, but you just can't let them get to you.

Chapter 13

Dealing with Colleagues

89.

Don't expect other teachers to support what you're doing.

I think you'll find that when you open up your curriculum to free choice reading other teachers feel a bit threatened. You're doing things differently than they are. Is that a comment on their teaching? And why are so many kids trying to get into your classes? You must just be easy.

This disapproval can be a very difficult thing to deal with, and I don't have any magic answers for you. I do know some things not to do.

90.

Don't expect other teachers to follow your lead.

They almost certainly won't, and then they'll become hostile on top of it. The only way I know of encouraging other teachers to move towards independent reading for their classes is to lead by example.

I do find that once teachers try a unit or two of student-selected books, they become much more open to the idea.

91. *Don't keep proselytizing.*

It's tempting, when you have a class full of excited readers and the other teachers are sitting at lunch complaining about how illiterate their kids are, to start telling about your classes. Don't. It will seem to them that you're bragging about your teaching ability, and there is simply no way to brag about your accomplishments without turning your audience off.

92. *Do try to keep up your friendships with other teachers.*

You do this for the simple, human reason that you need friends to function better at work. But you also do it because people will try new things that friends suggest when they won't touch something an administrator is trying to dictate. So be cool, keep your friends, and trust that sooner or later your example will convert some other teachers.

And if it doesn't? Well, you've helped the kids going through your classes, and it isn't given to many of us to change the world.

Chapter 14

Dealing with Administrators

93.

First, figure out exactly which administrator has the real power in your school.

It might be the principal, it might be your department chairman, it might be the superintendent. It will probably be the principal; notice who seems to be behind major changes.

94.

If the powerful administrator—we'll assume it's the principal—is someone with the students' interest firmly in the forefront, then you might try working with her.

It's great if you have administrative support, because then you'll get support for everything you do. You can probably get school funds for your classroom library, and the principal can help explain the program to any parents who have questions. Perhaps the principal will even visit your classroom, and tell about the books she's reading. Maybe she would encourage the secretaries, nurse, and guidance counselors to have books around their areas as well.

A supportive principal can also coax other teachers to allow some independent reading. I think many more teacher would do it, but they somehow think they will get in trouble for letting the kids spend class time reading.

95. *If there is any chance that your principal will say no to your independent reading program, then you should just quietly make your changes.*

Once a principal has refused permission for your changes, you're insubordinate if you go ahead, and that's usually grounds for firing. You don't want things to come to that. The idea is to get your program firmly in place before anyone notices and has a chance to forbid it.

96. *Once you have your students happily reading, your program is difficult to stop.*

You'll have parents happy with the reading, for one thing. You'll also have your students happy with the reading. Research is on your side; avid reading raises reading scores and most other scores as well.

If your principal complains, point out that you're still teaching the curriculum. Your students are still getting exposed to whatever classic books the school district has decided they should read.

They're just reading extra. What could be wrong with that?

And if your principal complains about the students sitting around "just reading" ask her if she minds if kids sit around "just doing math" or "just writing papers." What's the difference? What better thing could they be doing? Also point out that most kids have lives that are so scheduled now that they no longer read for pleasure at home. If it doesn't happen at school (in your class) then it doesn't happen at all.

97. *Point out how independent reading helps with all kinds of administrative problems, such as mainstreaming special ed. kids, parents trying to censor books, making special accommodations for gifted kids—all the things I've explained.*

I find that most administrators these days are so battered by the public and the politicians that they are really afraid of anything that is going to make waves. Your job—once your principal realizes what's going on—will be to convince her that her job is easier if you teach this way. With any luck you'll have been doing this for long enough that the benefits you mention will be obvious.

98. *Some principals never do seem to notice or care much about what's going on.*

If that's how your principal or department chairman is, be grateful for small blessings. Yes, it would be nice to have some support. And yes, it would be nice to hear a compliment now and again about what you're accomplishing. But you don't need that kind of help, and after awhile you'll feel very rewarded just by watching your students fall in love with books, and become literate people.

Chapter 15

Finally:

99. *Have fun yourself.*

I once saw a T-shirt with the slogan: "If the mother's not happy, ain't nobody happy." I think the same thing is true with teachers. If the teacher is not happy, no one is learning—or is learning all the wrong things. You want your students to understand, deep down in their essence somewhere, that reading is a fun, cool thing to do. You want them to respect, and maybe envy, your joy in books and learning.

So use these tips if they work for you. Or think up other ways of luring kids into the world of books. Whatever works. Whatever gets you up in the morning excited about going into school. Whatever brings that look of absorbed fascination on the face of your students as they read. Whatever gives you the satisfaction of knowing that, come hell or high water, you're doing the best you can for your classes.